Verses and Sc

Hilaire Belloc

Alpha Editions

This edition published in 2024

ISBN : 9789362921475

Design and Setting By
Alpha Editions
www.alphaedis.com
Email - info@alphaedis.com

As per information held with us this book is in Public Domain.
This book is a reproduction of an important historical work. Alpha Editions uses the best technology to reproduce historical work in the same manner it was first published to preserve its original nature. Any marks or number seen are left intentionally to preserve its true form.

Contents

VERSES...- 1 -
SONNETS...- 4 -
GROTESQUES..- 9 -
EPIGRAMS. ....- 15 -
SONNETS OF THE TWELVE MONTHS. ....- 17 -

VERSES.

THE NIGHT.

MOST holy Night, that still dost keep
The keys of all the doors of sleep,
To me when my tired eyelids close
Give thou repose.

And let the far lament of them
That chaunt the dead day's requiem
Make in my ears, who wakeful lie,
Soft lullaby.

Bid them that guard the sacred moon
By my bedside their memories croon;
So shall I have strange dreams and blest
In my brief rest.

Fold thy great wings about my face,
Hide day-dawn from my resting-place,
And cheat me with thy false delight,
Most holy Night.

HOMAGE.

I.

THERE is a light around your head

Which only Saints of God may wear,

And all the flowers on which you tread

In pleasaunce more than ours have fed,

And supped the essential air

Whose summer is a-pulse with music everywhere.

II.

For you are younger than the mornings are

That in the mountains break;

When upland shepherds see their only star

Pale on the dawn, and make

In his surcease the hours,

The early hours of all their happy circuit take.

CUCKOO!

IN woods so long time bare.

Cuckoo!

(Up in Mortain woods, I know not where)

Two notes fall.

Yet I do not envy him at all

His phantasy.

Cuckoo!

I too,

Somewhere,

I have sang as merrily as he

Who can dare,

Small and careless lover, so to laugh at care,
And who
Can call
Cuckoo!
In woods of winter weary,
In scented woods, of winter weary, call
Cuckoo!
In woods so long time bare.

SONNETS.

THE HARBOUR.

I WAS like one who grips the deck by night,
Bearing the tiller up against his breast;
I was like one who makes with all his might
For keeping course although so hardly prest;
Who veers with veering shock, now east, now west,
And strains his foothold still, and still makes play,
Of bending beams until the sacred light
Shows him high lands and heralds up the day.

But now such busy work of battle past,
I am like one whose barque at bar at last
Comes hardly heeling down the adventurous breeze,
And entering calmer seas,
I am like one that brings his merchandise
To Californian skies.

HER YOUTH.

YOUTH gave you to me, but I'll not believe
That youth will, taking his quick self, take you.
Youth's all our truth; he cannot so deceive;
He has our graces—not our own selves too.
He still compares with time when he'll be spent,
By human fate enhancing what we are;

Enriches us with dear experiment,
Lends arms to leaguered age in Time's rough war.

Look, this youth in us is an old man taking
A boy to make him wiser than his days.
So is our old youth our young ages making,
So rich in time his final debt he pays.
So with your quite young arms do you me hold,
And I will still be young when all the world's grown old.

LOVE AND HONOUR.

LOVE wooing Honour, Honour's love did win,
And had his pleasure all a summer's day.
Not understanding how the dooms begin,
Love wooing Honour, wooed her life away.
Then wandered he for full five years' unrest,
Until, one night, this Honour that had died
Came as he woke, in youth grown glorified,
And smiling like the saints whom God has blest.

But when he saw her in the dear night shine
Serene, with more than mortal light upon her,
The boy that careless was of things divine,
Small Love, turned penitent to worship Honour.
So Love can conquer Honour; when that's past,
Dead Honour risen outdoes Love at last.

HER MUSIC.

OH! do not play me music any more,
Lest in us mortal, some not mortal spell
Should stir strange hopes, and leave a tale to tell
Of two belovéd whom holy music bore,
Through whispering night and doubt's uncertain seas,
To drift at length along a dawnless shore,
The last sad goal of human harmonies.
Look! do not play me music any more.

You are my music and my mistress both,
Why, then, let music play the master here?
Make silent melody, Melodie. I am loath
To find that music, large in my soul's ear,
Should stop my fancy, hold my heart in prize,
And make me dreamer more than dreams are wise.

HER FAITH.

BECAUSE my faltering feet will fail to dare
The downward of the endless steps of Hell,
Give me the word in time that triumphs there.

I too must go into the dreadful hollow,
Where all our human laughter stops—and hark!
The tiny stuffless voices of the dark
Have called me, called me till I needs must follow.

Give me the word, and I'll attempt it well.

Say it's the little winking of an eye,

Which in that issue is uncurtained quite.
A little sleep that helps a moment by
Between the thin dawn and the large daylight.
Oh! tell me more than yet was hoped of men,
Swear that's true now, and I'll believe it then.

HER GIFT IN A GARDEN.

NOT for the luckless buds our roots may bear,
Now quite in bloom, now seared and cankered lying,
Will I entreat you, lest they should compare
My sad mortality with the fall of flowers;
But hold with me your chaste communion rare,
And touch with life this mortal case of ours.
For you were born beyond the power of dying:
I die as bounded things die everywhere.

You're full companionship, I'm silence lonely;
You're stuff, I'm void; you're living, I'm decay.
I fall, I think, to twilight ending only,
You lift, I know, to never-ending day.
And knowing living gift was life for me,
In narrow room of rhyme, I fixed it certainly.

THE CHECK.

SHALL any man for whose dear love another
Has thrown away his wealth and name in one,
Shall he turn scoffer of a more than brother,
To mock his needs when his desires are done?

Or shall a low-born boy whose mother won him
In great men great concerns his little place,
Turn, when his farthing honours come upon him,
To note her yeoman air and conscious grace?

Then mock me as you do my narrow scope,
For you it was put out this light of mine,
Traitrously wrecked my new adventured hope,
Wasted my wordy wealth, spilt my rich wine,
Made my square ship within a league of shore,
Alas! to be entombed in seas and seen no more.

THE POOR OF LONDON.

ALMIGHTY God, whose Justice, like a sun
Shall coruscate along the floors of heaven:
Raising what's low, perfecting what's undone,
Breaking the proud, and making odd things even.
The Poor of Jesus Christ along the street
In your rain sodden, in your snows unshod,
They have nor hearth, nor roof, nor daily meat,
Nor even the bread of men; Almighty God.

The Poor of Jesus Christ whom no man hears
Have called upon your vengeance much too long.
Wipe out not tears but blood: our eyes bleed tears:
Come, smite our damnéd sophistries so strong,
That thy rude hammer battering this rude wrong
Ring down the abyss of twice ten thousand years.

GROTESQUES.

NOËL.

I.

ON a winter's night long time ago
(*The bells ring loud and the bells ring low*),
When high howled wind, and down fell snow
(Carillon, Carilla).
Saint Joseph he and Nostre Dame,
Riding on an ass, full weary came
From Nazareth into Bethlehem.
And the small child Jesus smile on you.

II.

And Bethlehem inn they stood before
(*The bells ring less and the bells ring more*),
The landlord bade them begone from his door
(Carillon, Carilla).
"Poor folk" (says he) "must lie where they may,
For the Duke of Jewry comes this way,
With all his train on a Christmas Day."
And the small child Jesus smile on you.

III.

Poor folk that may my carol hear
(*The bells ring single and the bells ring clear*),
See! God's one Child had hardest cheer!

(Carillon, Carilla).

Men grown hard on a Christmas morn;

The dumb beast by and a babe forlorn.

It was very, very cold when our Lord was born.

And the small child Jesus smile on you.

IV.

Now these were Jews as Jews must be

(*The bells ring wild and the bells ring free!*),

But Christian men in a band are we

(Carillon, Carilla).

Empty we go and ill bedight,

Singing Noël on a winter's night;

Give us to sup by the warm firelight.

And the small child Jesus smile on you.

THE EARLY MORNING.

THE Moon on the one hand, the Dawn on the other;

The Moon is my sister, the Dawn is my brother.

The Moon on my left, and the Dawn on my right;

My Brother, good morning; my Sister, good night.

AUVERGNAT.

THERE was a man was half a clown

(It's so, my father tells of it),

He saw the church in Clermont Town,

And laughed to hear the bells of it.

He laughed to hear the bells that ring
In Clermont Church and round of it;
He heard the verger's daughter sing,
And loved her for the sound of it.

The verger's daughter said him nay
(She had the right of choice in it);
He left the town at break of day
(He hadn't had a voice in it).

The road went up, the road went down,
And there the matter ended it;
He broke his heart in Clermont Town,
At Pontgibaud they mended it.

THE WORLD'S END.

THE clouds are high and the skies are wide
(It's a weary way to the world's end).
I hear the wind upon a hillside
(Over the hills, away).

Over the hills and over the sea
(It's a weary way to the world's end).
The woman alone is a-calling me
(Over the hills, away).

Beyond the rim of the rising moon

(*It's a weary way to the world's end*).
He's back too late who starts too soon
(*Over the hills, away*).

He's wise, and he laughs who loves to roam
(*It's a weary way to the world's end*);
He's wise and he cries the when he comes home
(*Over the hills, away*).

Woman alone, and all alone
(*It's a weary way to the world's end*).
I'll just be sitting at home, my own,
The world's a weary way.

FILLE-LA-HAINE.

DEATH went into the steeple to ring,
And he pulled the rope and he tolled a knell.
Fille-la-Haine, how well you sing!
Why are they ringing the Passing Bell?
Death went into the steeple to ring;
Fille-la-Haine, how well you sing!

Death went down the stream in a boat,
Down the river of Seine went he;
Fille-la-Haine had a pain in her throat,
Fille-la-Haine was nothing to me.
Death went down the stream in a boat;
Fille-la-Haine had a pain in her throat.

Death went up the hill in a cart

(I have forgotten her lips and her laughter).

Fille-la-Haine was my sweetheart

(And all the village was following after).

Death went up the hill in a cart;

Fille-la-Haine was my sweetheart.

THE MOON'S FUNERAL.

THE Moon is dead. I saw her die.

She in a drifting cloud was drest,

She lay along the uncertain west,

A dream to see.

And very low she spake to me:

"I go where none may understand,

I fade into the nameless land,

And there must lie perpetually."

And therefore I,

And therefore loudly, loudly I

And high

And very piteously make cry:

"The Moon is dead. I saw her die."

And will she never rise again?

The Holy Moon? Oh, never more!

Perhaps along the inhuman shore

Where pale ghosts are

Beyond the far lethean fen

She and some wide infernal star—

To us who loved her never more,

The Moon will never rise again.

Oh! never more in nightly sky

Her eye so high shall peep and pry

To see the great world rolling by.

For why?

The Moon is dead. I saw her die.

THE JUSTICE OF THE PEACE.

DISTINGUISH carefully between these two,

This thing is yours, that other thing is mine.

You have a shirt, a brimless hat, a shoe

And half a coat. I am the Lord benign

Of fifty hundred acres of fat land

To which I have a right. You understand?

I have a right because I have, because,

Because I have—because I have a right.

Now be quite calm and good, obey the laws,

Remember your low station, do not fight

Against the goad, because, you know, it pricks

Whenever the uncleanly demos kicks.

I do not envy you your hat, your shoe.

Why should you envy me my small estate?

It's fearfully illogical in you

To fight with economic force and fate.

Moreover, I have got the upper hand,

And mean to keep it. Do you understand?

EPIGRAMS.

ON PERKINS—AN ACTOR.

PERKINS' Duchesses have marked a great
Improvement in his coster scene of late.
He gives the oath, the drunken lurch, the roar,
As even Perkins never did before.
And yet, the model is not far to seek—
Perkins was visiting at home last week.

ON SLOP—A POET.

WHERE Mr. Slop particularly shines
Is in his six sonorous single lines.
Perhaps where he is less successful is
In all the other verses. These are his.

ON TORTURE—A SINGER.

TORTURE has such an ear, I understand
He pays large sums to stop a German Band.
The public taste is quite a different thing,
Torture is positively paid to sing.

ON SUBTLE—A REVIEWER.

SUBTLE—your keen analysis and nice,
Like everything about you, has its price.

When you express your owner's private spite

A Pound rewards the virulence you write.

A Pound should therefore buy your praise; well, then,

Why should the Author have to pay you ten?

ON PAUNCH—A PARASITE.

PAUNCH talks about his Lady to excess,

And then about his curious Patroness,

And then he talks about himself, and then

We turn the conversation on to men.

ON PUGLEY—A DON.

PUGLEY denies the soul? Why, so do I

The soul, of Pugley, heartily deny.

SONNETS OF THE TWELVE MONTHS.

JANUARY.

IT freezes. All across a soundless sky
The birds go home. The horrible dark's begun:
The frozen dark that hopes not for a sun;
The ultimate dark wherein our race shall die.

Death, with his evil finger to his lip,
Leers in at human windows, turning spy
To learn the country where his rule shall lie
When he achieves perpetual generalship.

The undefeated enemy—the chill—
Which shall benumb the voiceful earth at last,
Is master of our moment, and has bound
The viewless wind itself. There is no sound.
It freezes. Every friendly stream is fast.
It freezes; and the graven twigs are still.

FEBRUARY.

THE winter moon has such a quiet car
That all the winter nights are dumb with rest;
She drives the gradual dark with drooping crest,
And dreams go wandering from her drowsy star.
Because her star is silent do not wake:
But there shall tremble on the general earth,

And over you, a quickening and a birth,
The sun is near the hill-tops for your sake.

The latest born of all the days shall creep,
To kiss the tender eyelids of the year,
And you shall wake, grown young with perfect sleep,
And smile at the new world, and make it dear
With living murmurs more than dreams are deep.
Silence is dead, my Dawn; the morning's here.

MARCH.

THE north-east wind has come from Norroway,
Roaring he came above the white waves' tips!
The foam of the loud sea was on his lips,
And all his hair was salt with falling spray.
Over the keen light of northern day
He cast his snow cloud's terrible eclipse;
Beyond our banks he suddenly struck the ships,
And left them labouring on his landward way.

The certain course that to his strength belongs
Drives him with gathering purpose and control
Until across Vendean flats he sees
Ocean, the eldest of his enemies.
Then wheels he for him, glorying in his goal,
And gives him challenge, bellowing battle-songs.

APRIL.

THE stranger warmth of the young sun obeying,
Look! little heads of green begin to grow,
And hidden flowers have dared their tops to show
Where late such droughty dusts were rudely playing.
It's not the month, but all the world's a-maying!
Come then with me, I'll take you, for I know
Where the first hedgethorns and white windflowers blow:
We two alone, that goes without the saying.

The month has treacherous clouds and moves in fears.
This April shames the month itself with smiles:
In whose new eyes I know no heaven of tears,
But still serene desire and between whiles,
So great a look that even April's grace
Makes only marvel at her only face.

MAY.

THIS is the laughing-eyed amongst them all:
My lady's month. A season of young things.
She rules the light with harmony, and brings
The year's first green upon the beeches tall.
How often, where long creepers wind and fall
Through the deep woods in noonday wanderings,
I've heard the month, when she to echo sings,
I've heard the month make merry madrigal.

How often, bosomed in the breathing strong
Of mosses and young flowerets, have I lain

And watched the clouds, and caught the sheltered song—
Which it were more than life to hear again—
Of those small birds that pipe it all day long
Not far from Marly by the memoried Seine.

JUNE.

RISE up, and do begin the day's adorning;
The Summer dark is but the dawn of day.
The last of sunset grows into the morning,
The morning calls you from the dark away.
The holy mist, the white mist of the morning,
Was wreathing upward on my lonely way.
My way was waiting for your own adorning,
That should complete the broad adornéd day.

Rise up, and do begin the day's adorning;
The little eastern clouds are dapple-gray,
There will be wind among the leaves to-day;
It is the very promise of the morning.
Lux tua via mea. Your light's my way:
Oh, do rise up and make it perfect day.

JULY.

THE Kings come riding back from the Crusade,
The purple Kings and all their mounted men;
They fill the street with clamorous cavalcade;
The Kings have broken down the Saracen.

Singing a great song of the eastern wars,
In crimson ships across the sea they came,
With crimson sails and diamonded dark oars,
That made the Mediterranean flash with flame.

And reading how, in that far month, the ranks
Formed on the edge of the desert, armoured all,
I wish to God that I had been with them
When the first Norman leapt upon the wall,
And Godfrey led the foremost of the Franks,
And young Lord Raymond stormed Jerusalem.

AUGUST.

THE soldier month, the bulwark of the year,
That never more shall hear such victories told;
He stands apparent with his heaven-high spear,
And helmeted of grand Etruscan gold.
Our harvest is the bounty he has won,
The loot his fiery temper takes by strength.
Oh! Paladin of the Imperial sun!
Oh! crown of all the seasons come at length!

This is sheer manhood; this is Charlemagne,
When he with his wide host came conquering home
From vengeance under Roncesvalles ta'en.
Or when his bramble beard flaked red with foam
Of bivouac wine-cups on the Lombard plain,
What time he swept to grasp the world at Rome.

SEPTEMBER.

I, FROM a window where the Meuse is wide,
Looked eastward out to the September night;
The men that in the hopeless battle died
Rose, and deployed, and stationed for the fight;
A brumal army, vague and ordered large
For mile on mile by some pale general;
I saw them lean by companies to the charge,
But no man living heard the bugle-call.

And fading still, and pointing to their scars,
They fled in lessening cloud, where gray and high
Dawn lay along the heaven in misty bars;
But watching from that eastern casement, I
Saw the Republic splendid in the sky,
And round her terrible head the morning stars.

OCTOBER.

LOOK, how those steep woods on the mountain's face
Burn, burn against the sunset; now the cold
Invades our very noon: the year's grown old,
Mornings are dark, and evenings come apace.
The vines below have lost their purple grace,
And in Forrèze the white wrack backward rolled,
Hangs to the hills tempestuous, fold on fold,
And moaning gusts make desolate all the place.

Mine host the month, at thy good hostelry,

Tired limbs I'll stretch and steaming beast I'll tether;
Pile on great logs with Gascon hand and free,
And pour the Gascon stuff that laughs at weather;
Swell your tough lungs, north wind, no whit care we,
Singing old songs and drinking wine together.

NOVEMBER.

NOVEMBER is some historied Emperor,
Conquered in age, but foot to foot with fate,
Who from his refuge high has caught the roar
Of squadrons in pursuit, and now, too late,
Stirrups the storm and calls the winds to war,
And arms the garrison of his last heir-loom,
And shakes the sky to its extremest shore
With battle against irrevocable doom.

Till, driven and hurled from his strong citadels,
He flies in hurrying cloud; and spurs him on
Empty of lingerings, empty of farewells
And final benedictions, and is gone.
But in my garden all the trees have shed
Their legacies of the light, and all the flowers are dead.

DECEMBER.

HOAR Time about the house betakes him slow,
Seeking an entry for his weariness;
And in that dreadful company, Distress

And the sad Night with silent footsteps go.
On my poor hearth the brands are scarce aglow,
And in the woods without pale wanderers press;
Where, waning in the pines from less to less,
Mysterious hangs the hornéd moon, and low.

For now December, full of aged care,
Comes in upon the year and weakly grieves,
Mumbling his lost desires and his despair;
And with mad, trembling hand still interweaves
The dank sear flower-stalks tangled in his hair,
While round about him whirl the rotten leaves.

Milton Keynes UK
Ingram Content Group UK Ltd.
UKHW042146281024
450365UK00010B/671